ART DECO
LIGHTING

HERB MILLMAN AND JOHN DWYER

880 Lower Valley Road, Atglen, PA 19310 USA

Designed by Bonnie M. Hensley
Cover design by Bruce M. Waters
Type set in Copperplate Gothic BD BT/Aldine 721 BT

ISBN: 0-7643-1357-6
Printed in China
1 2 3 4

Published by Schiffer Publishing Ltd.
4880 Lower Valley Road
Atglen, PA 19310
Phone: (610) 593-1777; Fax: (610) 593-2002
E-mail: Schifferbk@aol.com
Please visit our web site catalog at **www.schifferbooks.com**

In Europe, Schiffer books are distributed by Bushwood Books
6 Marksbury Avenue Kew Gardens
Surrey TW9 4JF England
Phone: 44 (0) 20-8392-8585; Fax: 44 (0) 20-8392-9876
E-mail: Bushwd@aol.com
Free postage in the UK. Europe: air mail at cost.

This book may be purchased from the publisher.
Include $3.95 for shipping. Please try your bookstore first.
We are always looking for people to write books on new and related subjects.
If you have an idea for a book please contact us at the Atglen, PA., address.
You may write for a free catalog.

CONTENTS

Acknowledgments

This book has been a labor of love for two years; it is nice to know that dreams can come true. We took our hobby of collecting art deco and turned it into a business nearly five years ago. Now this book has resulted.

We first acknowledge the tremendoous support we have received from the New Hope community. A special thank you goes to those who have supported us in our business and allowed us to photograph items which came from our shop: Mr. & Mrs. Robert MacDonnell of New Jersey; Terry McCloughan and Donald Toner of Pennsylvania; Michael & Lisa Hlatke of New Jersey who have been loyal supporters since the opening of our business; Axel Wieschenberg of New Jersey who has supported our efforts for the past four years; and Richard Bockman, owner of Torpedo Art Glass in Summerville, New Jersey, who served as glass consultant.

Many other clients have given us continued support and we could fill many pages with their names; you know who you are and we are grateful.

A special thank you also goes to our family and friends whose continuing support has helped us come this far. Fran Dwyer and Abe Millman are not here to share this book with us, but we know they are proud of us. Lastly, we thank three special friends who were our driving force and always believed in us: Les Sdorow, Janice Landgraf, and Amanda Kimball.

We must also take this opportunity to thank Peter and Nancy Schiffer. Without their confidence, guidance, and patience, we would never have had the opportunity to create this book.

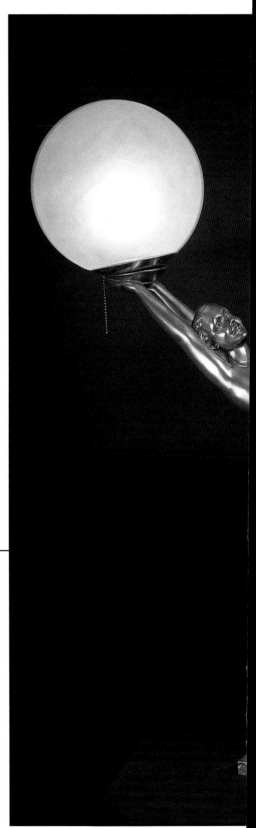

PREFACE

We came, we saw, we purchased. That was the motto we lived by as we became more involved in the acquisition of art deco items. We had been collectors for over 20 years when we made our avocation our vocation. We opened our store, Cockamamie's in New Hope, Pennsylvania, on the Fourth of July in 1996. It was natural for us to gravitate toward the deco style, considering our backgrounds. Herb was involved in the motion picture industry for 27 years, becoming vice-president of a New York City movie circuit. John graduated with a bachelor of fine arts in theater acting and acted off Broadway and regionally. If you love the theatre and the movies, how could you not love deco?

Before the 1980s ushered in the multiplexes and box-like arts centers, there were lush movie palaces with over-the-top grandeur and many deco touches. What are remembrances for us, are remembrances for many. When people come into our shop, many memories are evoked; whether from their own experiences with "what grandma had at home" or from going to movie theatres where 1930s chandeliers and sconces announced you were having a special night. Movie-going was an event where the decor was an important part of the experience. Passing under an elaborate and large chandelier in the lobby, going along the grand staircase with lush carpeting and impressive sconces, we settled into plush seats with our dates and our popcorn. Whether we saw them first-run or on television reruns, we were transported into fantasy worlds of the 1920s, '30s, and '40s where Fred Astaire dances in top hat and tails with Ginger Rogers at the El Morocco or the Stork Club, Myrna Loy and William Powell mix martinis, and a myriad of other romantic stars live the sophisticated life amid deco opulence.

Besides the higher-end deco that exemplified America's new-found wealth and international prominence in the 1920s, there were mass-produced pieces that were available to all. These came to be known as "depression modern" and made full use of new materials and technology. Many pieces contain chrome or Bakelite, and many of them ended up in our livingrooms.

Hopefully, this book will help you to evaluate relative overall quality and price ranges for art deco lighting. Please note, however, that in any antique store, the proprietor is regaled by stories about what people paid for a piece. Weekly, on the television "Antiques Roadshow," we see people surprised by what their "antique" is appraised for. The price ranges given here are retail values that reflect our special niche in art deco lighting and are what we would sell the piece for in our store. If you are bequeathed a piece or find one at a yard sale for a pittance, you have been lucky. Also, prices vary from one location to another. As deco is an urben style, there is greater supply and demand for it in New York, the Miami region, and California. In these areas prices may be high, but also there is greater abundance of high-end pieces. Art deco is highly collectible and comparatively affordable. Happy hunting!

INTRODUCTION

LIGHTING THROUGH THE YEARS

It is said that when someone has an idea, "a light bulb goes on." In fact, the reverse is also true: "the light bulb going on" was a great idea. Prior to the invention of the electric light bulb, people lit their homes with candles, oil and kerosene lamps, and gas fixtures.

The invention of the light bulb in America is attributed to Thomas A. Edison in 1879. There is truth to that, but to give all the credit due we should go back to the earlier 1800s. In 1808, at London's Royal Institute, Sir Humphrey Davy exhibited a carbon arc lamp. Two pieces of carbon were set apart and an electrical current was passed through a circuit that included the carbon. When the current reached the carbon, the electricity jumped from one piece to the other, creating an arc. This electric light had many problems, however. The light was irregular because the carbon could not maintain its position as it burned. Also, the carbon burned too fast and too bright for practical use.

In the mid-1840s, Edward Staite and others worked on developing artificial light with two platinum wires inside a glass bulb. Between the wires they placed a carbon filiment that glowed (or incandesced) when electric current passed through it. When air got to the filament, the carbon would disintegrate (burn), blackening the inside of the bulb. The problem then was in making a vacuum in the bulb.

The invention of the mercury vacuum pump by Hermann Sprengel of Germany, in 1865, was the beginning of the solution to the vacuum problem. The practical application of these inventions toward developing a light bulb was acheived by Sir Joseph Swan of England in 1878. However, it was Edison's bulb in 1879 that burned longer and more steadily that gained more commercial value.

After the electric light bulb was proven successful, a whole new world of inventions followed, including new designs for electrical lighting.

Manufacturers began producing elaborately designed chandeliers and wall sconces for use in commercial spaces, such as theaters, office buildings, restaurants, and museums. Only very wealthy individuals could afford to have electrical lighting in their homes initially.

Through the 1920s and to the end of the art deco period in the 1940s, manufacturers produced new lighting fixtures through mass production at a rapid rate and at affordable prices. The supply met the demand. Gradually, electrical lighting spread to private homes everywhere. Incredible chandeliers, wall sconces, and table lamps, that as gas lights decades ago were more limited in their designs, became more ornate and impressive. Besides lights for general illumination and reading, there developed interest in accent lighting. Limitless design opportunities were acheived through electrical lighting.

The electrification of interior lighting had a profound effect on society. New lighting was brighter, cheaper, and safer than old methods. The concept of a "work" day and a "play" night were forever altered. The new way of lighting ushered in new ways of living.

In the art deco era, lamps that were not used for general illumination were considered novelties, such as radio lamps, figural lamps, and lighted smoking stands. Today, these same are considered collectible forms of utilitaraian art. In the new millenium, art deco style lighting is being installed in new theaters, restaurants, and hotels as a means to capture the aura of stylish days gone by. The sleek designs, grace, and sophistication of the art deco period, that is associated also with the famous dancing of Fred Astaire, is conveyed in the lighting and furnishings of that time. It is little wonder that art deco lighting has become desirable again and, like Mr. Astaire, has danced its way into the hearts and homes of a new generation.

CHAPTER 1
ACCENT AND FIGURAL RADIO LAMPS

From the 1920s through the 1940s, electrically-powered accent and figural lamps were designed with intricate detail and manufactured in Europe and America. Two companies in America, Frankart and Nuart, became distinguished manufacturers of figural table lamps. These lamps often included a sculptured figure, such as a female nude, cast from white metal or bronze. Both the figure and the lamp were designed to sit on a common base. They were used as accent s throughout the home and frequently were placed on the family's large radio cabinet. There these lamps would emanate light throughout the room as the family sat and raptly listened to variety shows, comedy sketches, and mystery theaters. The name "radio lamp" was thus coined.

As well as the more typical female figures, other lamp manufacturers' designs of this era included male figures, birds, deer, dogs, elephants, gazelles, and other animals—all with a sense of movement. The lamps were made at a massive rate and demand was high. They had a craftsman-like appearance and their subjects reflected sophisticated and exotic designs that appealed to the public's sense of high class and good taste. They were substantial in weight and made to last.

The lamps were accompanied by a variety of glass globes from Czechoslovakia which served as their shades. Many shades were multi-faceted and colorful and were often marked "Czech" on their inner rims. Original Czech shades today are extremely desirable and are sold separately at good prices. Many other vintage shades were made in America.

1920s Parlor Lamp
White metal with a bronze wash, circular marble base, and multi-colored Czechoslovakian glass globe of the deco period. 21" high x 5 1/2" diameter. $1,350 - $1,500

Late 1920s Accent Lamp
A rare lamp of white metal with a bronze wash. Original curved slag glass on all sides and on lid. 11 3/4" high x 4 1/8" diameter. $465 - $595

1920s European Figural Lamp
One-of-a-kind, magnificent lamp constructed of white metal with a pewter finish. There are some brass highlights on the lamp as well. The figure is standing on an Italian marble base. The globe is a very rare oversized European crackle glass. 38" high x 13 1/2" wide base.
$2,500 - $3,400

Late 1920s to early 1930s Dual Figural Radio Lamp
The base has an intricate and exquisite geometric design. The female nudes flanking the light have Egyptian influence. The original glass was pale green bubble glass; this is replacement glass. White metal with a light green wash, a color popular for lamps and accessories from the 1920s through the 1940s. 12" high x 10" wide. $850 - $1,150

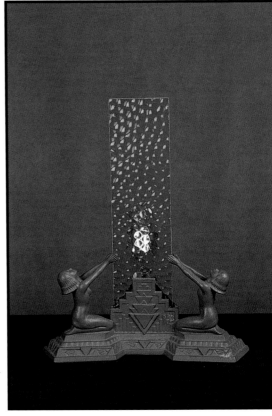

Late 1920s or early 1930s Figural Accent Lamp
Female figures over orange Czechosolovakian glass. Base of white metal. Rare. 7 1/2" high x 3" diameter. $395 - $485

Late 1920s or early 1930s Figural Accent Lamp
White metal with bronze wash and with very intricate detail. Original flame glass globe white frosted with hint of yellow. 22" high x 5" wide. $475 - $600

Late 1920s Figural Lamp

Unusual in both its size and design, the focal point of this lamp is the female figure which stands beneath a glass dome with border of scalloped design. The dome is supported by three columns of Greek design. Base and dome made of white cased glass with a raised design. The female figure of white metal with a bronze wash. The face is ivory. The three metal columns were constructed of white metal with a white finish. 14 1/2" high x 6" diameter . $850 - $1,125

Early 1930s Figural Accent Lamp
Base and dome of alabaster, surrounding columns and female figure are white metal with gold tone wash and face is white resin. 14 1/2" high x 7" diameter of base. $1,050 - $1,200

Egyptian Bronze Figural Accent Lamp

This outstanding bronze lamp has a black finish with gold accents. The shades are swirled carnival glass. European or American. This is the second such lamp we have seen; the first had a green patina and two similar carnival glass shades. 16 1/2" high x 13 1/4" wide. $1,850 - $2,600

Early 1930s Accent Lamp
Solid Alabaster in an unusual design. 14 1/8" high x 4" square base. $585 - $695

1940s Accent Lamp
Base is satin frosted glass with three chrome-plated rods which support the shade. The frosted glass shade has been replaced. 15 1/4" high x 5 1/4" wide. $195 - $250

1930s Figural Accent Lamp
White metal with a bronze wash. Shade has been replaced. 10 1/4" high. $410 - $525

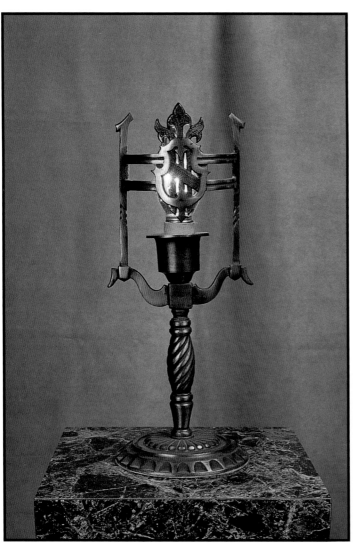

1930s Accent Lamp
Solid brass with intricate design. 13" high x 5 1/4" wide. $365 - $445

1930s Figural Accent Lamp
This lamp was designed to rest at the bottom post of a stairwell banister. White metal with a bronze wash and multi-colored frosted glass shade. These lamps have a number of different finishes with a variety of glass globes. The glass shade on this lamp is hard to find. 20" high x 4 1/2" wide. $465 - $550

1930s Figural Accent Lamp
White metal with bronze wash. Intricate design throughout the lamp base. Period shade of white frosted glass. 17" high x 9 1/4" wide. $465 - $585

1930s Accent Lamp
Designed with architectural detail and three glass cylinders joined. Shade of frosted, pale green glass with a satin finish resting on a white metal base with black baked-on finish. 8 1/2" wide x 7 1/2" high. $485 - $575

1930s Figural Accent Lamp
Figure and base of white metal with black and gold wash. Milk glass cylinder with chrome cover containing four air holes for heat release. 9 3/4" high x 5 3/4" wide x 7 1/4" deep. $545 - $675

1930s Figural Accent Lamp
White metal with chrome-plating. The cylinder shade of white milk glass with chrome plated lid that has air holes to let heat escape, thus preventing the shade from cracking from the heat. 10" high x 5" wide. $550 - $690

Opposite page: **1930s Female Figural Accent Lamp**
Figure and base constructed of white metal with chrome plating. The cylinder milk glass shade has horizontal ribs at its upper section and a stepped top. 5" wide x 10" high. $565 - $620

1930s Figural Accent Lamp
This classic figural accent lamp has a female figure of white
metal that had been chrome plated. The figure rests on a milk
glass cube which has a geometric design on all four sides. 9 3/4"
high x 3 1/2" square base. $340 - $495

1930s Figural Accent Lamp
The weeping nude figure of white metal with a
pewter finish stands on a white milk glass cube. 7"
full height, milk glass cube 3 1/2" square. $385 - $450

1930s Figural Accent Lamp
White metal with a pewter wash. The figure stands
on a molded white frosted glass cube which has a
satin finish. The detail in the glass is very subtle.
3 1/2" cube base / 9 1/4" high. $465 - $525

1930s Figural Accent Lamp
Female figure of chrome plate on a
white milk glass cube. Overall Height
7 3/4", figure 4 1/2" high, base 3 1/4"
square. $385 - $490

Early 1930s Radio Lamp
Fine detailed white metal female figure
with bronze and pewter finish on a base
of multi-colored alabaster. The head is
faux ivory. 12 1/2" high x 5 3/4" base.
$775 - $1,100

1930s Figural Accent Lamp
Bronze with multi-colored finish.
Glass has been replaced. 14 1/2" high
x 7 1/4" wide. $865 - $990

1930s Figural Accent Lamp
This unusual gold-tone washed white metal lamp
has a female figure flanked by two vertical mirrors. The light is cast from vertical frosted glass
which rests between the mirrors, enabling the
figure to be seen from all angles. 7" wide x 7 1/2"
high. $420 - $525

1930s Figural Lamp
Cast figure with bronze wash. Blasted
red glass has been replaced. 15 1/2" high
x 5" wide. $495 - $610

1930s Figural Accent Lamp
Plaster with a bronze wash displaying Egyptian influence and intricate detail. White frosted glass insert has been replaced. 11" high x 6 1/4" wide. $395 - $510

1930s Figural Accent Lamp
White metal. Blue bubble glass is a replacement. This lamp is now being reproduced with a variety of finishes. 15 1/2" high x 5" wide. $365 - $475

1930s Figural Accent Lamp
White metal and cast iron. Figure has original green patina while base is black. Glass has been replaced. 9 1/2" high x 8 1/2" wide (with glass insert). $415 - $600

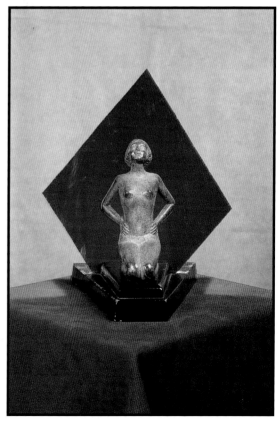

1930s Figural Accent Lamp
Figure riding a dolphin. White metal with white finish on the figure
and black base. Lamp has been restored with new colors. The flame-
shaped shade is period. 9" wide x 10 1/2" high. $495 - $610

1930s Figural Radio Lamp
Figure and base of white metal with black finish. Alongside the figure is Czechoslovakian end-of-the-day glass. This rare globe is unusual with a prominent mixture of blue blended with other subtle colors. 11 1/2" wide x 11 1/4" high. $585 - $710

1930s Female Figural Accent Lamp
Unusual design in white metal with a restored pale green finish. The Czechoslovakian multi-colored glass globe is unusual in color. 12 1/2" wide x 10 3/4" high . $495 - $650

Early 1930s Figural Accent Lamp
White metal with gold-tone wash. Multi-colored Czechoslovakian end-of-the-day glass globe. 19 1/2" high x 4 1/4" wide. $445 - $565

Early 1930s Figural Accent Lamp
Spelter with a pewter wash. Multi-colored Czechoslovakian end-of-the-day glass globe. 23" high x 5 1/4" wide. $415 - $550

1930s Figural Accent Lamp
Unusual detail appears in white metal with bronze and gold-tone wash. Czechoslovakian glass globe. 11 1/2" wide x 18" high x 5 1/2" in depth. $565 - $725

1930s Figural Accent Lamp
White metal with pewter finish and intricate detail throughout the base. Czechoslovakian multi-colored glass globe. 14 1/2" high x 5 3/4" wide. $465 - $575

1930s Figural Accent Lamp
Bronze on a marble base with a period Czechoslovakian glass globe. 21 1/4" high x 6 1/4" diameter of marble base. $985 - $1,100

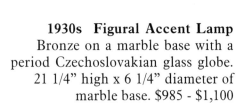

1930s Figural Accent Lamp
Figure standing on the head of a serpent in white metal with nickel-plate. Flame globe has been replaced. 18 1/2" high x 6 1/2" wide. $365 - $480

1930s Figural Radio Lamp
Lady on the moon, composition white metal with a bronze wash. Unusual globe of multi-layered frosted cream glass from the 1930s period. 6 1/2" wide x 17" high. $485 - $600

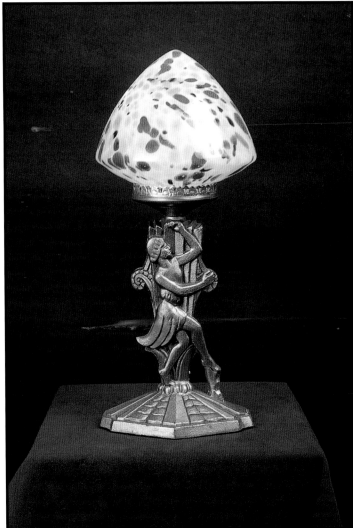

1930s Nuart Figural Accent Lamp
White metal with a black wash made by Nuart.
Multi-colored satin glass globe is of the 1930s
period. 12" high on 3" wide base. $535 - $600

1930s Figural Accent Lamp
White metal with gold-tone wash. Intricate design
throughout the base with red and green highlights.
Multi-colored Czechoslovakian glass globe of
unusual design. 13 3/4" high x 5 3/4" wide at base.
$565 - $650

1930s Figural Accent Lamp
Detailed figure of a nude mermaid in white metal with bronze wash. Globe of pale green satin glass. This is a rare lamp. 14 1/2" high x 6 1/4" wide. $565 - $650

1930s Nuart Figural Radio Lamp
This is a classic Nuart figural design, one of their most popular figures that appeared not only on lamps but also on ashtrays and bookends. White metal with a black finish. This lamp has lost most of its original finish and a great deal of the original white metal is exposed. The period globe is a frosted pale green flame with an intricate design throughout the glass. 8 1/2" wide x 7 1/2" high. $645 - $800

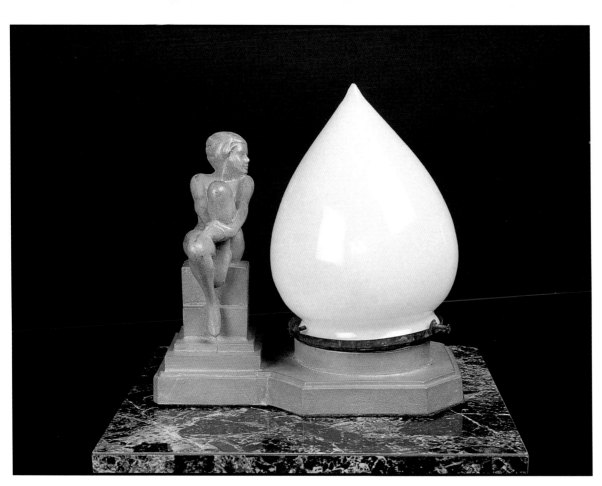

1930s Nuart Figural Radio Lamp
The figure is seated with the typical pose of the era. Made by Nuart from white metal with its original green patina which has some discoloration. The period globe is an unusual inverted teardrop shape of pale yellow glass. 8" wide x 7 1/4" high. $685 - $800

1930s Nuart Figural Radio Lamp
This classic radio lamp was designed by Nuart in their traditional pose. White metal with a pewter wash. The period green satin glass shade is not usual in design. 8" wide x 6 1/2" high. $685 - $795

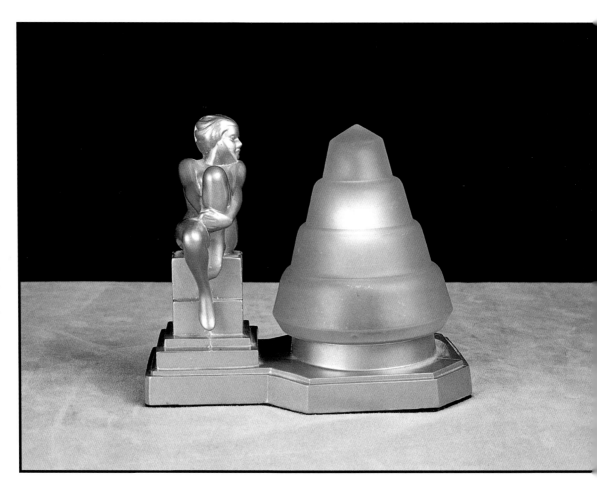

1930's Female Figural Accent Lamp
Spelter with a pewter finish. The period frosted amber glass shade has a vertical ribbed design. 8" wide x 6 3/4" high. $450 - $575

1930s Nuart Figural Radio Lamp
White metal with a bronze wash. Over the years much of the original finish has deteriorated which now has exposed the white metal. This figure is seated with the traditional pose. The seeded glass globe is rare and seldom seen. 8 1/4" wide x 6 1/2" high. $685 - $790

1930s Figural Radio Lamp
White metal with bronze wash. Globe of green "brain glass." 11 1/2" wide x 8 1/4" high. $425 - $510

1930s Figural Accent Lamp
Plaster with bronze and gold tone wash. Bubble glass ball with flat bottom used to diffuse light. 8 1/4" wide x 8 3/4" high. $490 - $575

1930s Figural Accent Lamp
Figure and base are chalk composition. The lamp
has Egyptian influence with a green brain glass
globe from the deco period. 5 1/2" wide x 13"
high. $395 - $445

1930s Figural Accent Lamp
White metal with black finish. The pale green
brain glass globe is deco period. The figure is
holding a Fenton glass cigarette box. 6" wide x
12 1/2" high. $610 - $745

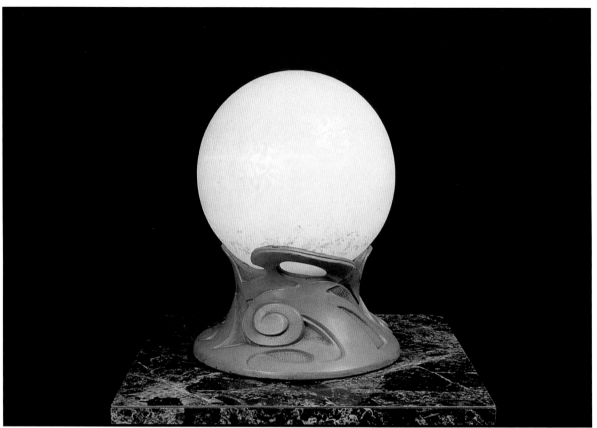

Early 1930s Accent Lamp
White metal with light green finish. Base and globe are unusual in design. Globe is American made with unusual glass. 9 1/4" high x 6 1/8" diameter base. $495 - $600

1930s Figural Radio Lamp
White metal with a silver/pewter finish. The figural rests on a black marble base. The globe is a European crackle glass. 15" high x 6" wide. $675 - $925

Early 1930s Figural Accent Lamp
White metal with a pewter wash. This magnificent lamp is one-of-a-kind. The detail of the figure and stepped base make it a treasure. The oversized vintage crackle glass globe is the perfect finishing touch. 6 1/2" square base x 24" high. $785 - $1,000

1930s Figural Accent Lamp
White metal with chrome plate. This lamp is rarely seen. The female figure is kneeling and reclining. The base is black marble with four chrome balls supporting the base which are not original to the lamp. The globe is a spectacular crackle glass which appears to be of the deco period. 13 1/2" wide x 15 1/2" high. $950 - $1,475

1930s Figural Lamp with Egyptian Influence
Cast metal with gold tone wash. Globe of
Czechoslovakian glass. 21" high x 5 1/4" square
base. $865 - $950

1930s Accent Lamp with Egyptian Influence
White metal with bronze wash. The globe is multi-
colored Czechoslovakian glass. 6" wide x 18 1/2"
high. $495 - $585

1930s Figural Radio Lamp with Egyptian Influence
White metal with bronze wash. Czechoslovakian multi-colored glass globe. 14 3/4" high x 3 5/8" wide at base. $465 - $590

1930s Nuart Figural Radio Lamp
White metal with black finish. Multi-colored Czechoslovakian glass globe. This is one of the traditional Nuart lamp designs. 7 1/2" high x 9 1/2" wide. $595 - $765

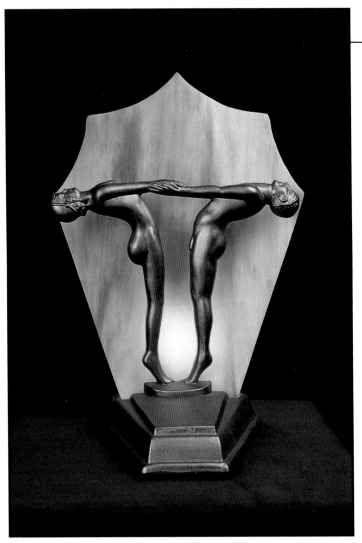

1930s   Dual Figural Accent Lamp
This unusual lamp has two female nudes holding hands while leaning backward.
White metal with gold-tone wash. The glass has been replaced. 10" high x 7 3/4" wide. $495 - $550

Early 1930s Gondola Dual Figural Radio Lamp
Cast plaster with a gold-tone wash. This Gondola lamp is most unusual in style. The amber crackle glass vertical shade is rarely seen. When lit, the shade emits a beautiful spectrum of gold tones through the crackle glass. 9 1/4" high x 13" wide.
$395 - $520

Early 1930s Dual Figural Radio Lamp
Spelter with bronze wash. This classic lamp has two female nudes seated back to back. Between them rests an unusual four-sided vertical amber crackle glass shade. 8 3/4" high x 11 1/2" wide.
$565 - $685

Early 1930s "Gondola" Dual Figural Radio Lamp
White metal with black finish. The white metal shows through the black, possibly from exposure or excessive cleaning. Amber rain glass globe. 12" wide x 6 1/2" high.
$265 - $350

1930s Dual Figural Radio Lamp
White metal with gold tone wash. Figures kneeling back-to-back on marble base. Amber crackle glass globe of the deco period. 14" wide x 6 1/4" high. $725 - $850

1930s Dual Figural Lamp
White metal with bronze wash. Figures are mandolin players. Czechoslovakian multicolored glass globe. 11 3/4" wide x 8 1/4" high. $495 - $565

1930s Dual Figural Radio Lamp
White metal with bronze wash. Multi-colored Czechoslovakian glass globe. 7 1/2" high x 10 3/4" wide. $540 - $625

Early 1930s Dual Male Figural Lamp
Base and center globe of alabaster. The figures are white metal with bronze gold-tone wash. The globe splits at the center to allow access to the bulb. 14 1/4" wide x 5 1/8" high. $950 - $1,200

1930s Dual Figural Radio Lamp

White metal with black finish. Two standing female figural nudes back-to-back. Between them rests an amber crackle glass globe of the deco period. The base has a geometric design throughout. 9 1/2" wide x 8 1/2" high. $495 - $675

1930s Dual Figural Accent Lamp

White metal with pewter wash. The base is cast with a black finish. Between the nude figuress rests a multi-colored satin glass globe of the deco period. $410 - $500

1930s Dual Figural Accent Lamp
White metal figures and base cast metal with dark, gold-tone wash. Unusual artistic lamp designed with two nude female figures standing back-to-back. Between the figures rests a globe with a lattice design. Various shades of slag glass and amber bubble glass line the lamp's interior. 10 1/2" wide x 9" high. $495 - $600

1930s Dual Figural Radio Lamp
White metal with aged bronze wash and some light discoloration on base. Frosted pressed glass shade. 10 1/2" high x 12" wide. $445 - $580

1930s Dual Figural Radio Lamp
White metal with pewter wash. The housing that
holds the old flame globe has been replaced. 8 1/4"
wide x 12 3/4" high. $495 - $655

1930s Dual Figural Accent Lamp
White metal with black finish. This unusual lamp
is on an Italian black marble base. Amber crackle
glass tiered shade. The rare globe is seldom seen.
15 1/2" high x 9 1/2" wide. Base diameter 6 1/2".
$685 - $825

1930s Dual Figural Radio Lamp
White metal with bronze wash. End-of-day
Czechoslovakian glass globe. 11" wide x 15" high x
3 1/2" in depth. $675 - $750

1930s Tri-Figural Accent Lamp
White metal with bronze wash. Czechoslovakian multi-colored end-of- day Czechoslovakian glass globe. 18 1/4" high x 6 1/4" wide.
$690 - $845

Opposite page:
1930s Dual Figural Accent Lamp
White metal with bronze wash. Green crackle
glass globe. 11 1/2" high x 6" wide. $435 - $520

1930s Dual Figural Radio Lamp
White metal with gold-tone wash. The figures
have been painted. Multi-colored Czechoslovakian glass globe. 12" high x 7 1/2" wide.
$425 - $495

1930s Dual Figural Radio Lamp
White metal with a gold-tone wash. Unusual globe
of multi-toned alabaster. The globe separates at the
center to allow access to change the bulb. The lower
portion of the alabaster globe is affixed to the lamp
base, while the upper portion lifts up. Air hole at
top of the globe to allow the heat to escape so the
alabaster will not overheat. 11 1/4" high x 4 3/4"
diameter of the base. $685 - $800

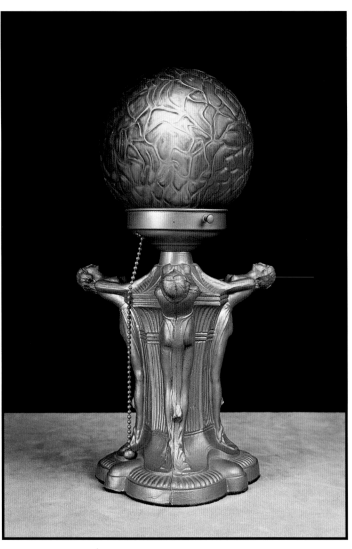

1930s Tri-figural Accent Lamp
White metal with gold-tone wash. The amber
brain glass globe is of the deco period. 7" wide x
13 1/2" high, $565 - $710

1930s Dual Figural Accent Lamp
White metal with bronze wash. Green bubble satin
glass globe. 11 1/2" high x 5 3/4" wide. $495 - $600

1930s Dog Figural Accent Lamp
White metal with a bronze wash. German Shepherd dog sits high on the lamp base. The light is recessed to the right of the dog. The globe is pressed bubble glass designed for this lamp. 8" wide x 9" high. $495 - $600

1930s Elephant Figural Accent Lamp
White metal with black finish. Crackle glass globe has been replaced. Elephant trunks in an upward position means Good Luck. 6" high x 8 3/4" wide. $325 - $385

1930s Eagle Figural Accent Lamp
White metal with pewter wash. Amber glass globe of the deco period. 7" high x 7 1/4" wide. $295 - $350

1930s Charriott Accent Lamp
White metal with gold-tone wash. Intricate detail throughout base. Amber brain glass globe. 12" high x 11 1/2" wide. $395 - $470

1930s Gazelles Dual Figural Radio Lamp
White metal with a silver-green wash. This most unusual lamp has two gazelles joined at the center. The geometric design throughout the base adds to its overall design. The Czechoslovakian glass globe is multi-colored. 12 1/4" wide x 11 1/4" high. $595 - $710

1930s Eagle Dual Figural Radio Lamp
White metal restored with an iridescent, soft green finish. Two eagles with spread wings flank a green, brain glass globe. 10 1/2" wide x 8 1/4" high. $425 - $510

Opposite page:
1940s Seal Figural Lamp
Plaster with pewter wash. Transparent pale
green globe of the deco period. 15" high x 6"
wide. $395 - $480

1940s Quadra-figural Tiffen Glass Accent Lamp
The original lamps of this style were manufactured
in the 1920s. This four-sided lamp has a figure on
each side. The glass globe rests on a black metal
base. This lamp has its original cloth wiring.
These lamps are currently being reproduced. 10"
high x 5" square. $450 - $525

Early 1940s Accent Lamp
Multi-toned alabaster with geometric design cut in.
Upper portion of the pyramid separates from the
base to allow access for bulb replacement. 10 1/2"
high x 4" diameter of base. $395 - $485

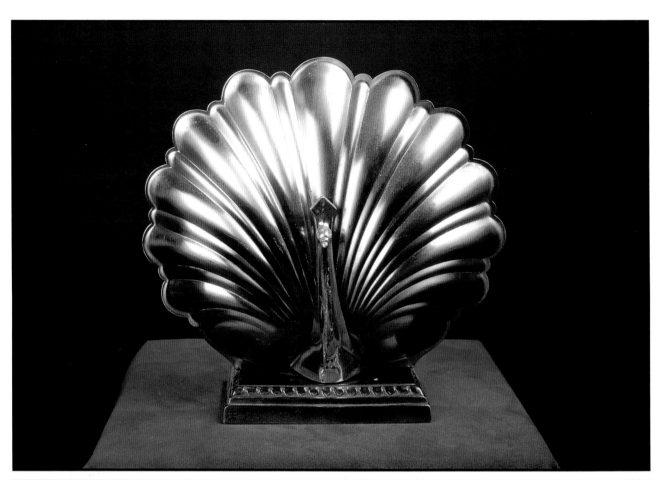

1940s Peacock Lamp
The peacock and feathers are copper on a cast iron base. The peacock's feathers defuse the light from behind. 11 3/4" wide x 12 1/4" high. $310 - $425

1940s Dog Accent Figural Lamp
Ceramic. Light socket installed in mouth gives the appearance
of the dog holding a ball. 5 1/2" high x 8" wide. $75 - $115

Chapter 2
Table Lamps

When electric table lamps were first manufactured worldwide, most were unsigned by the makers; little did they realize that signed pieces might be more valuable seventy years later. Art deco style lamps were durably constructed of brass, bronze, cast iron, and ceramics. Over the years, for safety reasons, the original wiring may have been changed and fabric or parchment shades may have been replaced, since daily use and cleaning may have caused the original shades to become worn.

Opposite page:
1920s Figural Table Lamp
White metal and bronze. Head dress, bodice, and shoes are bronze and skirt is white metal. Base is marble and brass. Hands and face are a resin composition. Very rare, hard-to-find lamp. Shade has been replaced. 17 1/2" high x 5 3/4" wide. $1,250 - $1,800

1920s Table Lamps
White metal with bronze wash. Very intricate design. Original paper shades welded onto the back of the frames. 16" high x 7 3/4" wide x 4" deep. $565 - $620 pair

1904-1910 European Table Lamps with Egyptian Influence
Solid brass with intricate detail. Original fabric shades are removable. 27 1/2" high x 7 1/4" base. $1,125 - $1,300 pair

Late 1920s Three-Piece Ensemble
White metal and brass. This classic ensemble consists of two
reverse painted lamps and a center compote. The dome
above each lamp has its original hinge which allows access
to the bulb by swinging the dome backwards. The zig-zag
sculptured design surrounding the painted glass panels adds
to their charm. The compote has flying dragons on either
side. The three pieces have a gold-tone black wash and brass
accents. Lamps 18" high x 6 1/4" square base. Compote 10"
high x 15" wide x 6" square base. $1,035 - $1,250

1930s European Table Lamps
Porcelain with glazed and bisque finishes. 21"
high x 6" diameter base. Shades have been
replaced. $795 - $900 pair

1930s Chase Desk Lamp
Chrome housing and base with glass shade.
$145 - $210

1930s Chase Desk Lamp
Chrome frame and base. Glass shade of the deco period. $145 - $195

**1930s Vanit[y]
Lamp**
Geometric
brass base w[ith]
mirror inset[.]
Chrome-plat[ed]
shade with
glass beaded
fringe. 17"
high x 4 3/4"
wide.
$325 - $400

1930s Table Lamp
Base is plaster with intricate detail of three elephants with trunks pointed up for good luck. Shade is Kokomo glass with original silk fringe. 29" high x 8 3/4" diameter base. $790 - $950

1930s Desk Lamp
Chrome with original pull chain switch. $295 - $385

1930s Table Lamp
White metal chrome-plated. Architectural design in base. 24" high x 7 1/2" diameter base. $695 - 875

1930s Table Lamp
Cast iron with black wash and architectural design in base. Original European crackle glass globe. 24" high x 8" diameter base. $685 - $850

Opposite page:
Top: **1930s Alabaster Table Lamps**
Alabaster. 13 1/2" diameter x 4 1/4" square base. $795 - $950

Bottom: **Early 1940s Accent Table Lamps**
Spun aluminum. Shades have a dark blue accent border and Bakelite finial.
Stars with midnight blue enamel filler are cut in the aluminum around the
lower section of each base. 9" high x 2 3/4" diameter base. $465 - $595

 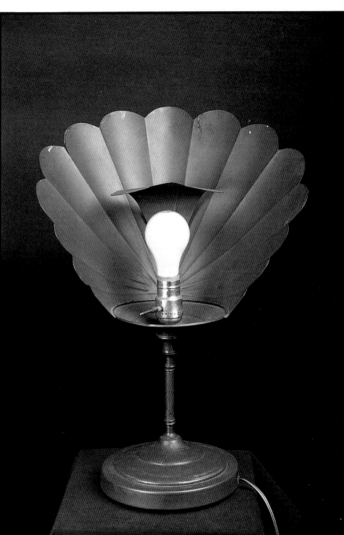

1940s Accent Table Lamp
Copper. 19" high x 14" width x 8" diameter of base
$295 - $350

Many movie classics with 1920s through 1940s settings show the heroine seated in front of her vanity table in the light of a pair of boudoir lamps. These lamps were somewhat delicate in design and feminine. Unfortunately, over the years, many original boudoir lamps have become broken and pairs are nice to find today.

1930s Boudoir Lamps
Bases of clear pressed and cobalt blue frosted glass. Shades are blue frosted glass with intricate design and original chrome finials. 13" high x 5" wide base. $495 - $585 pair

1930s Skyscraper Boudoir Lamp
Bakelite base and finial, and Celluloid. Great skyscraper design. 21" high x 8" diameter base. $545 - $595

1930s Boudoir Lamp
Base and removable cover are chrome plated. Glass shade of ribbed frosted glass. 10 3/4" high x 4" diameter base with Bakelite switch. $195 - $265

Opposite page:
1930s Boudoir Lamps
Chrome bases with removable chrome
tops. Glass shades are white frosted with
intricate design. 11 1/2" high x 3 3/4"
diameter base. $295 - $375 pair

1930s Boudoir Lamp
Base of etched frosted glass. Shade is ribbed frosted
glass with aluminum housing and finial. 9" high x
4 1/2" wide base x 2 3/4" deep. $295 - $375

1940s Boudoir Lamp
White metal base with pewter finish. Cylinder shade
with bubble blue satin glass and intricate deco
design. 11 3/4" high x 4 3/4" base. $145 - $190

 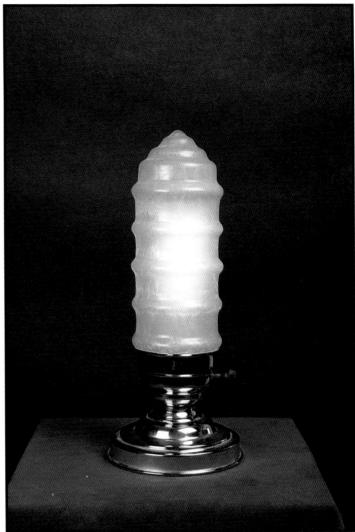

1940s Boudoir Lamp
Frosted glass shade with aluminum base. Pull
chain switch. 11 3/4" high x 4 1/2" diameter base.
$120 - $165

1940s Boudoir Lamp
Chrome plated base. Woven cream colored
frosted glass shade. 11 1/2" high x 4 1/2"
diameter base. $120 - $165

1940s Boudoir Lamp
Pressed glass base with Bakelite housing for light socket. Orange frosted glass shade. 11" high x 4" diameter base. $145 - $190

1940s Boudoir Lamp
Base and shade pressed glass with intricate deco design and Bakelite housing. 11 3/4" high x 4" diameter. $165 - $195

1940s Boudoir Lamp
Pressed glass base with chrome housing
for light socket. Pressed glass cylinder
shade. 11" high x 4 1/2" diameter base. -
$120 - $140

1940s Boudoir Lamp
Cylinder base and shade of white frosted satin glass
with chrome plated accents. 14" high x 4 1/2" diameter base. $175 - $220

1940s Boudoir Lamps
Bases and removable tops manufactured of spun aluminum. The glass shades are frosted pressed glass with an intricate deco design. 11 3/4" high x 4 1/2" diameter base. $265 - $350

1940s Boudoir Lamps
Base is bubble pressed glass. The shades are a powder blue with clear glass tops and a criss-cross web design. 12" high x 4" diameter base. $235 - $310

**1940s Bou-
doir Lamps**
The shades
a frosted sa
glass with
rounded top
of unusual
design. The
bases are
chrome pla
with black
accents. 11"
high x 5"
diameter ba
$495 - $585

1940s Boudoir Lamps
The shades are woven blue frosted glass on chrome plated bases. 1 1/2" high x 4 1/2" diameter base. $285-375

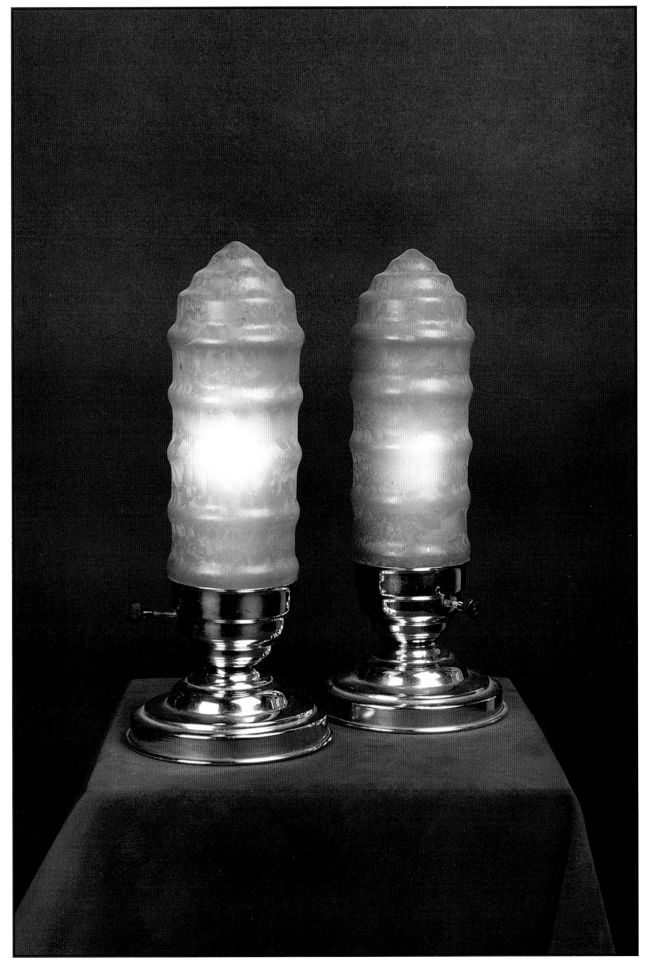

CHAPTER 3
OVERHEAD AND WALL LIGHTING

Commercial establishments in the 1920s through the 1940s were the first buildings adorned with art deco wall sconces, ceiling fixtures, and chandeliers. Lobbies of office buildings, theaters, and restaurants had these elegant fixtures. Gradually, there was increased demand for this lighting in homes.

1920s European Wall Sconces
Solid brass with intricate detail. Note griffin at
upper portion. Flame globe has been replaced.
$995 - $1,150

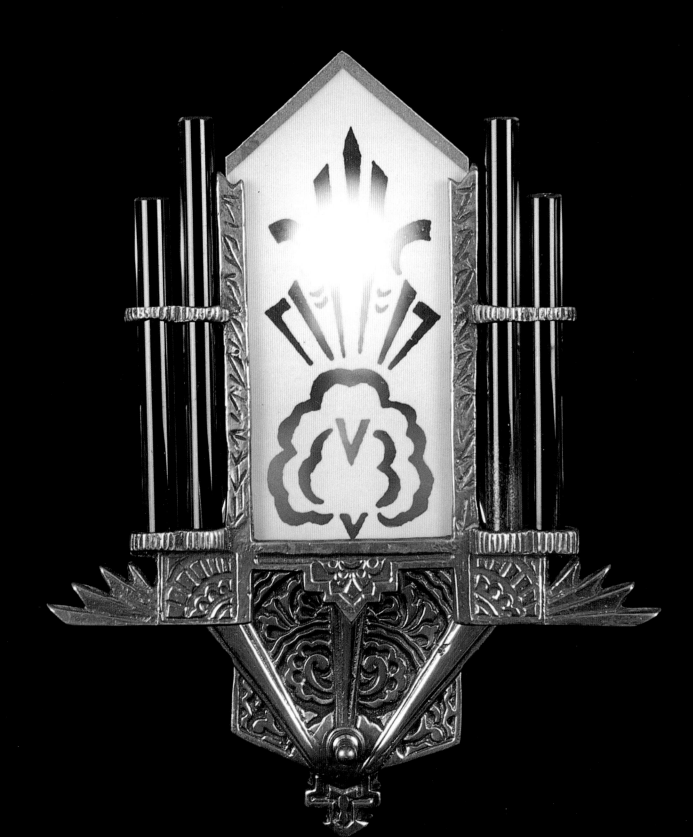

Opposite page:
1920s Slip Shade Panel Wall Sconce
White metal with nickel plate. Achitectural design in back plate. White frosted glass panel with clear etchings at center. Original amber and green glass rods flank center panel. $799 - $899

1930s Wall Sconce
White metal chrome plated. 19" high x 20 1/2" wide. $495 - $575

1930s Slip Shade Wall Sconce
White metal chrome plated. Slip shade is frosted white. $399 - $425

1930s Oversized Wall Sconce
White metal with copper plate.
$405 - $465

Early 1930s Slip Shade Wall Sconces
White metal with pewter wash. Each back plate
has intricate detail with separate on/off switch.
Slip shades are white frosted with vertical deco
design. $875 - $999 pair

Early 1930s Slip Shade Wall Sconces
White metal with pewter finish and original red and blue paint at top and bottom. Intricate design throughout back plates. Slip shades amber in color, fading from light to dark. Shades also have intricate design. $899 - $999 pair

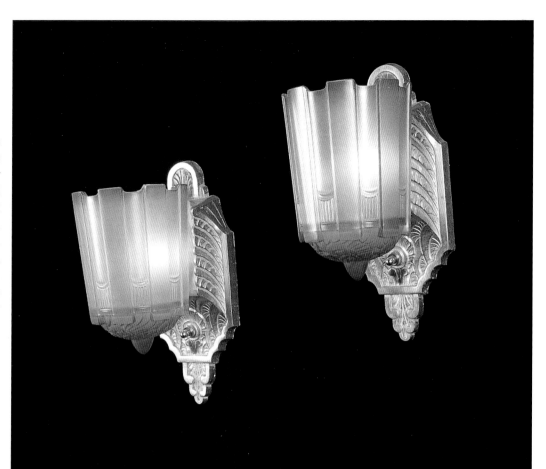

Early 1930s Slip Shade Wall Sconces
White metal with pewter finish. Slip shades deep amber color. $899 - $995 pair

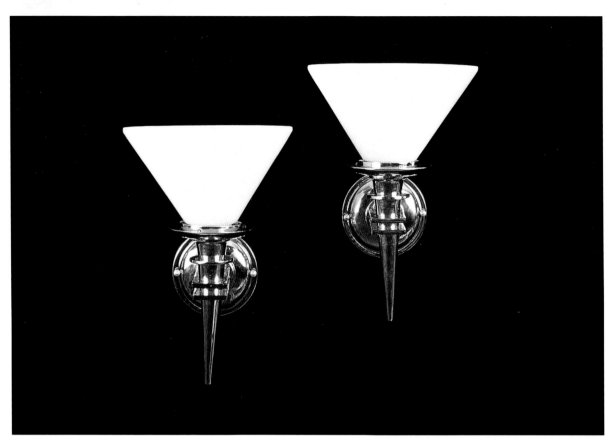

1930s Wall Sconces
White metal nickel-plated. Original white milk
glass shades. $795 - $900 pair

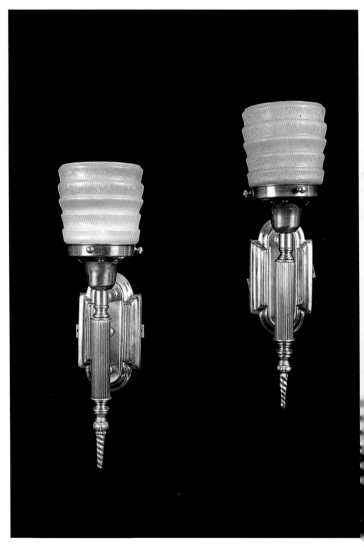

1930s Wall Sconces
Brass with intricate design throughout.
Deco period glass shades pink with hori-
zontal ribs throughout. $495 - $610 pair

1930s Candle Wall Sconce
White metal with black and gold-tone wash. $195 - $245

1930s Candle Wall Sconces
White metal with gold-tone
wash. $345 - $375 pair

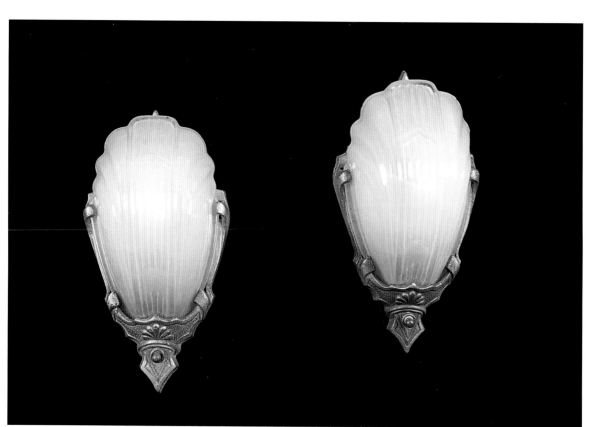

1930s Slip Shade Wall Sconces
White metal with gold-tone wash. Each back plate has a separate on/off switch. Slip shades are amber colored glass with chevron design. When turned off, slip shades appear as carnival glass. $789 - $899 pair

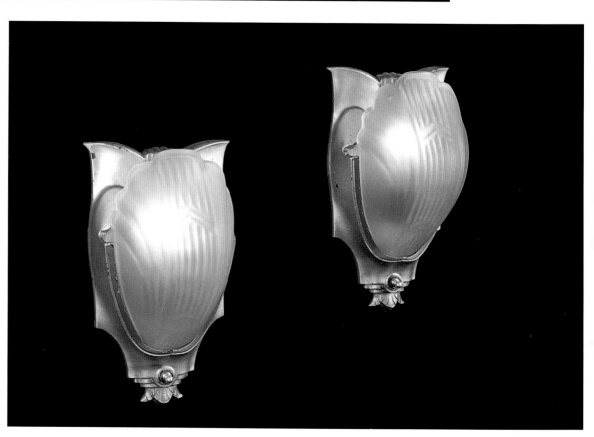

1930s Slip Shade Wall Sconces
White metal with pewter finish. Slip shades of frosted white glass with chevron design. $799 - $899 pair

Early 1930s   Slip Shade Wall Sconces
White metal with gold wash. Intricate design in back plates.
Slip shades are deep amber in color. $849 - $999 pair

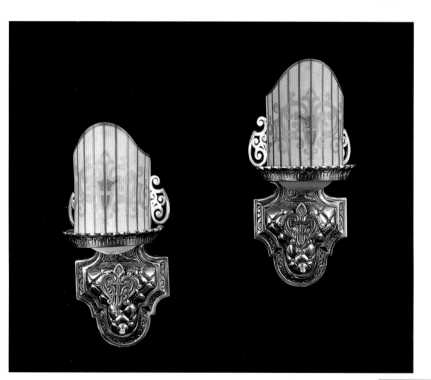

Early 1930s Beardslee Slip Shade Wall Sconces
White metal with pewter wash. Intricate design in back plates. Slip shades are multi-colored cream with vertical bands. $899 - $1,099 pair

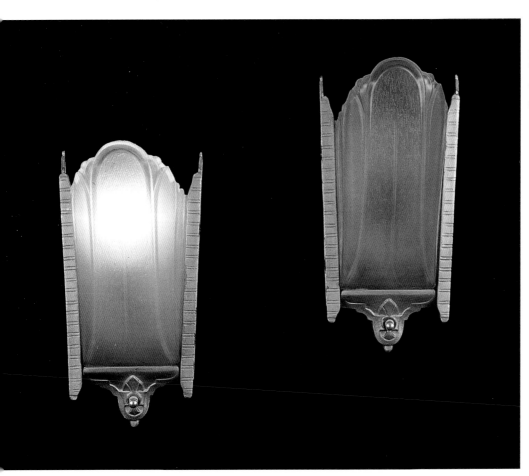

1930s Slip Shade Wall Scones
White metal with gold-tone wash. Slip shades are amber satin glass. $899 - $975 pair

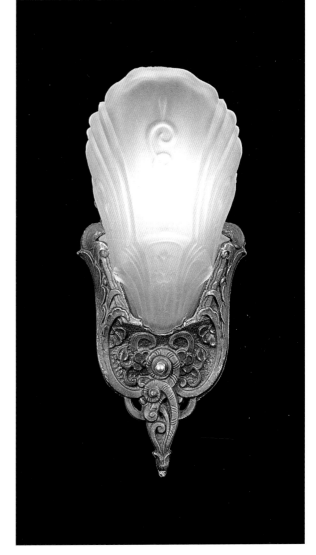

Early 1930s Slip Shade Wall Sconce
White metal with bronze wash. Slip shade is amber in color. $385 - $435

1930s Single Sconce
Sconce with three flat glass
inserts. $310 - $375

Opposite page:
Top: **Early 1930s Slip Shade
Wall Sconces**
White metal with bronze wash.
Slip shades are pale amber in
color. $785 - $999 pair

Bottom: **1930s Wall Sconces**
Chrome. Glass shades are cream
in color. $499 - $575 pair

**Early 1930s Slip
Shade Wall
Sconces**
White metal with
bronze wash.
Consolidated
glass shades
amber in color.
$899 - 1,100 pair

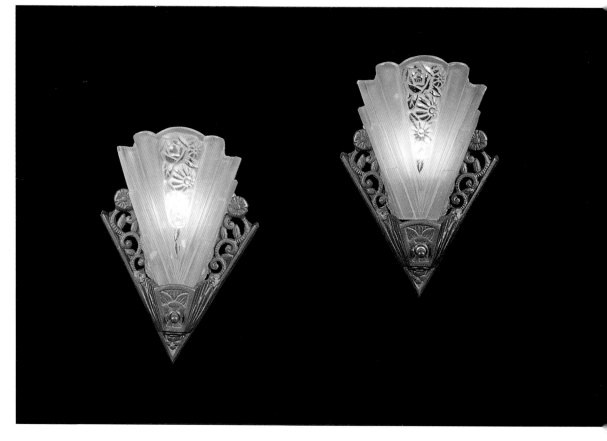

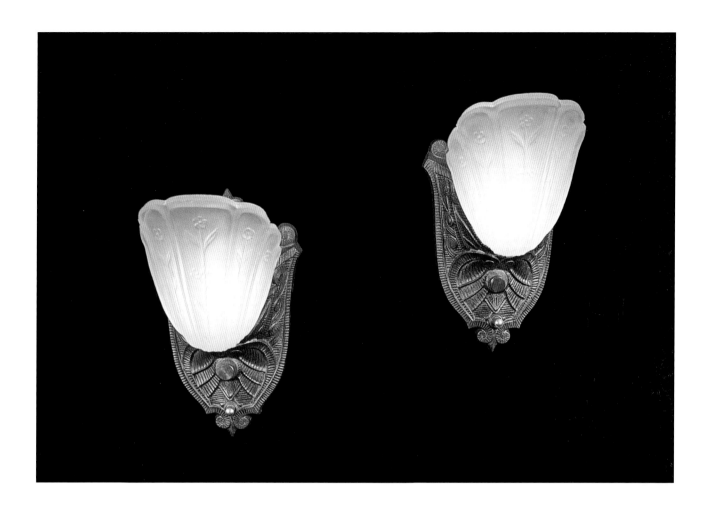

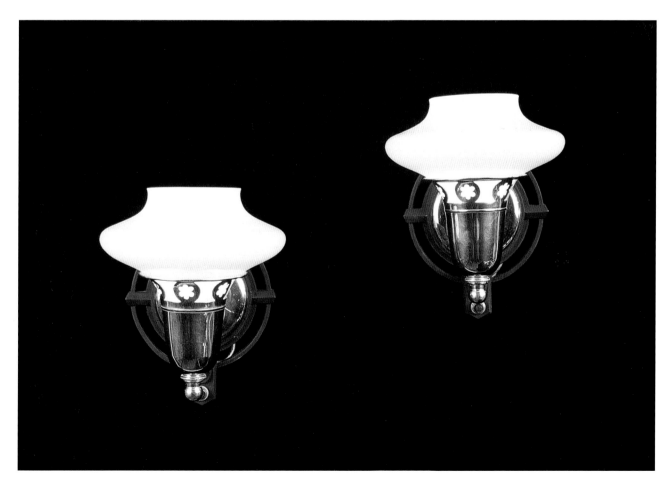

1930s Slip Shade Wall Sconces
Solid brass with curlicues above shades. Glass shades are cream in color. $485 - $550 pair

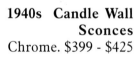

1940s Candle Wall Sconces
Chrome. $399 - $425

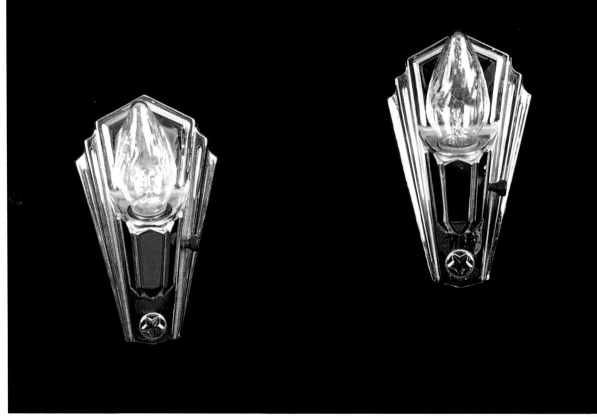

1940s Candle Wall Sconce
White ceramic. Original pull chain.
$235 - $275

**1940s Wall
Sconces**
Ceramic with
pink iridescent
finish. Separate
on/off switch on
each sconce.
$395 - $485 pair

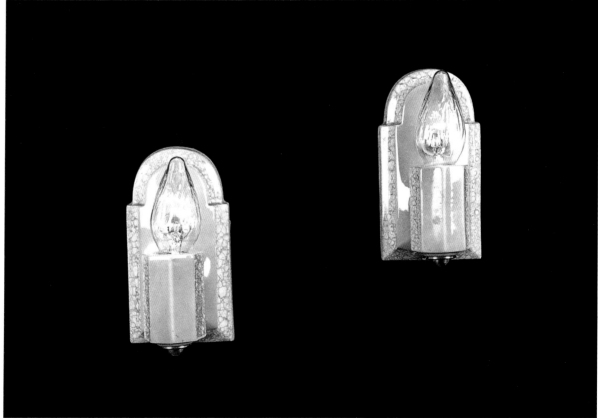

Opposite page:
1940s Wall Sconces
Chrome. Each sconce has a separate on/off
switch and electrical receptacle. Glass shades
are a combination of white milk glass with
frosted square at center. $445 - $500 pair

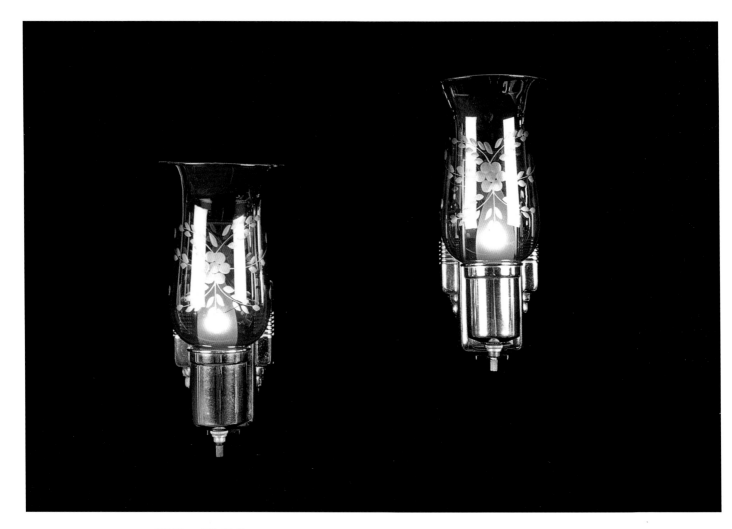

1940s Wall Sconces
Chrome. Replaced shades are cranberry etched glass. $435 - $495 pair

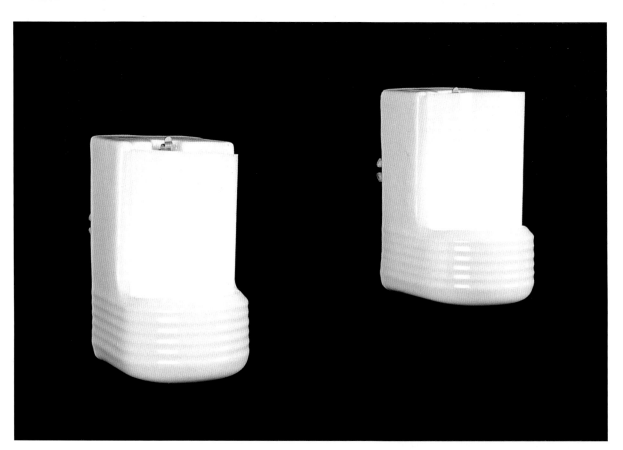

1940s Wall Sconces
White ceramic. Shades are white milk
glass cylinders. $399 - $465 pair

1940s Wall Sconce
Ceramic with black finish.
Shade is white milk glass
cylinder. $249 - $285

1940s Wall Sconces
White metal with gold-tone wash. Glass shades are curved with floral
design embossed at center. $399 - $450 pair

1910 European End-of-Day Glass Ceiling Fixture
Canopy, housing, and fitter are solid brass. End-of-day glass is mutli-color cream and caramel. $599 - $725

1920s Slag Glass Ceiling Fixture
White metal with cream finish. Slag glass panels are cream color. $499 - $525

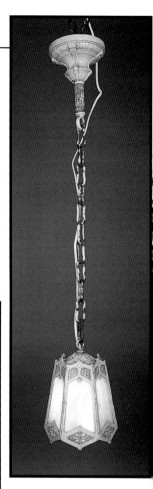

Early 1920s European Ceiling Fixture
Composition of frame is black wrought iron. Woven crystal throughout. $1,195 - $1,400

1920s French Five-Light, Slip Shade Chandelier
Frame white metal with black finish. Four slip shades and bottom plate are white frosted glass. $2,400 - $2,950

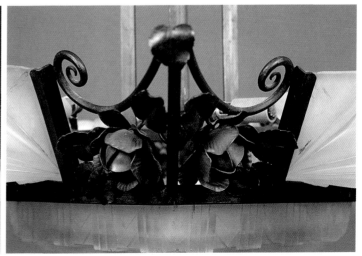

Early 1930s Slip Shade Ceiling Fixture
White metal with bronze wash. Flush mount fixture. Slip shades are light cream in color with caramel accents. $899 - $985

1930s Pink Glass Ceiling Fixture
$325 - $365

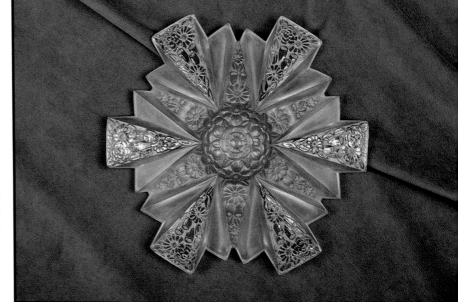

1930s Pale Green Glass Ceiling Fixture
$325 - $365

1930s Three-Light Ceiling Fixture
White metal with pewter finish. Intricate detail throughout. $375 - $449

1930s Three-Light Ceiling Fixture
White metal with bronze wash. Intricate detail throughout.
$265 - $325

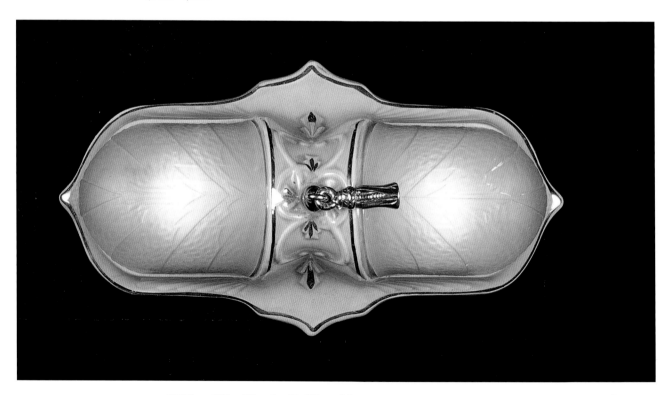

1930s Slip Shade Ceiling Fixture
Ceramic, pale green in color, Slip shades are pale green.
$499 - $565

1930s Five Light Slip Shade Chandelier
Chrome with brass accents. Slip shades are white frosted with intricate design in shades.
$1,299 - $1,499

1930s Pendant Ceiling Fixture
Brass canopy, housing, and fitter. White milk glass with black design embossed. $495 - $545

1930s Halophane Ceiling Fixture
Chrome canopy, housing and fitter. $445 - $499

1930s Pendant Ceiling Fixture
Chrome ceiling canopy, housing, fitter, and band.
Fixture is white milk glass with pressed clear glass
bottom plate. $550 - $610

1930s Halophane Ceiling Fixture
Chrome canopy, housing, and band. 33" high x
9" diameter x 7" fitting. $465 - $525

1930s Ceiling Fixture
Brass frame with original white glass panels
throughout. 35" high. $799 - $925

1930s Ceiling Fixture
Brushed aluminum with brass accents. White milk
glass cylinder insert. Fixture 37" high. Additional
aluminum rods extend 6 feet. $799 - $859

1930s Ceiling Fixture
White milk glass with black design embossed
throughout. $495 - $550

1930s Ceiling Fixture
White milk glass with black design embossed throughout. $495 - $550

1930s Ceiling Fixture
White milk glass with design embossed over glass panels. $449 - $485

1930s Ceiling Fixture
White frosted glass. $425 - $499

1940s Ceiling Fixture
White milk glass with black ribbed vertical
design. $495 - $550

1940s Ceiling Fixture
White milk glass with black vertical and geometric accents. $495 - $525

1940s Ceiling Fixture
White milk glass and clear pressed glass. Black vertical and geometric design on white milk glass with pressed glass bottom plate. $395 - $425

1940s Pendant Ceiling Fixture
White milk glass and pressed glass. $395-445

1940s Ceiling Fixture
Pink frosted glass with a deco design throughout.
$399-425

1940s Ceiling Fixture
Amber frosted and pressed glass.
$285-325

1940s Ceiling Fixture
White frosted and pressed
glass. $275-299

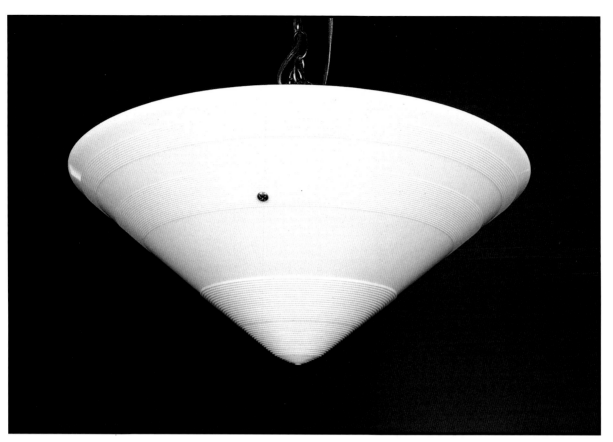

1940s Ceiling Fixture
White milk glass with raised deco design throughout. $395 - $445

1940s Ceiling Fixture
Original brass-fitted column and
ceiling canopy. White milk glass
with clear pressed glass. Deco
design. $445 - $499

1940s Ceiling Fixture
White metal with pewter wash. Glass shade
amber colored. $495 - $550

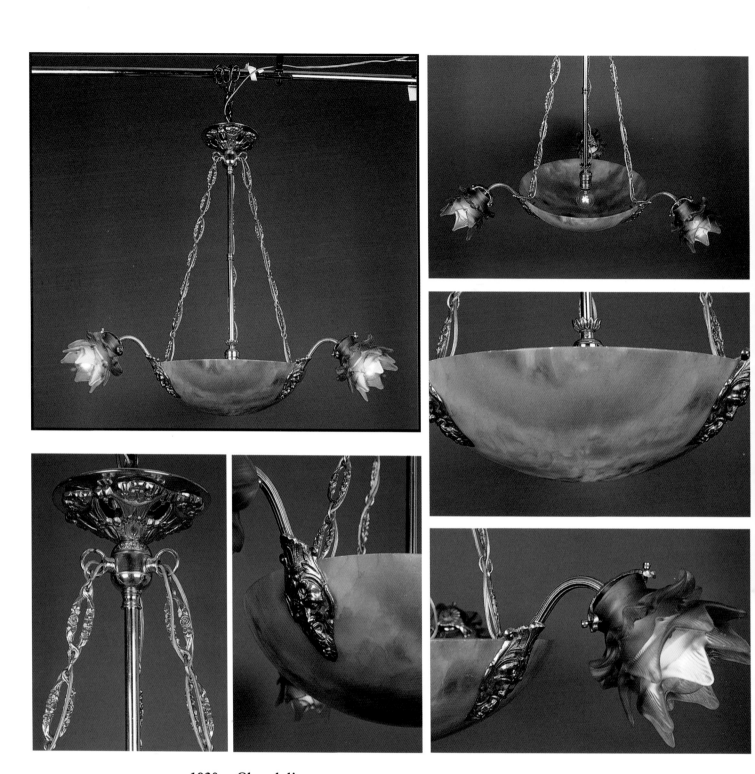

1920s Chandelier
Alabaster bowl of amber color with three amber satin glass
florets protruding. All accents, including the three chains
which suspend the fixture and the ceiling canopy, are solid
brass. $1,799 - $2,250

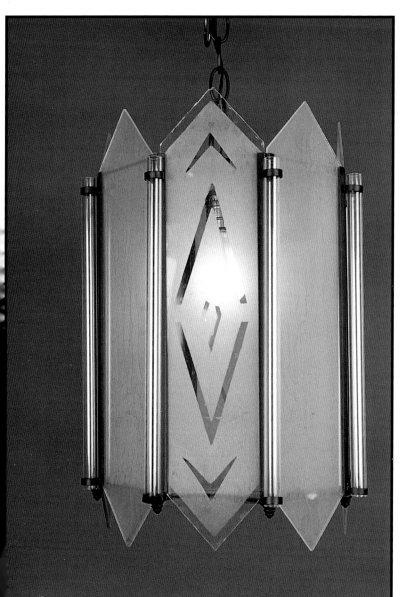

1920s Ceiling fixture
Frosted etched glass panels
with clear glass rod inserts.
$699 - $745

1920s Slip Shade Chandelier
White metal with bronze wash.
Mica inserts at points where
shades meet. Slip shades are amber
color. $799 - $950

121

Early 1930s Three-Light Slip Shade Chandelier Solid bronze. Slip shades vary from light amber to dark amber in color. This style was also made with five lights. $1,199 - $1,499

1930s Seven Light Slip Shade Chandelier
Bronze. Slip shades and bottom plate have ribbed vertical design.
Flush mount. $1,125 - $1,295

**1930s Five-Light Slip
Shade Chandelier**
Copper. Slip shades are
white frosted. $995 - $1,075

1930s Three Light Slip Shade Chandelier
White metal with gold-tone wash. Slip shades are white frosted. $699 - $785

1930s Five-Light Slip Shade Chandelier
White metal with bronze wash. Slip shades are amber in color with floral design in center. $1,299 - $1,325

1930s Five-Light Slip Shade Chandelier
Brass and Bakelite. Chandelier has a three-way turn switch at base. Slip shades are pale cream in color with caramel accents. $999 - $1,150

Bottom left & right: **1930s Five-Light Slip Shade Chandelier**
White metal with gold-tone finish and intricate design. Slip shades are amber in color with chevron design embossed. When turned off, shades appear as carnival glass. $995 - $1,150

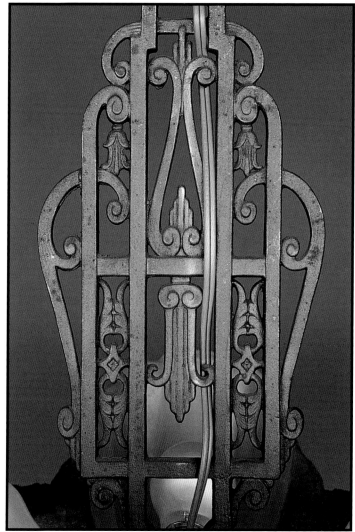

1930s Five-Light Slip Shade Chandelier
White metal with gold-tone wash. Slip shades
are white frosted in color. $799 - $899

1930s Five Light Slip Shade Chandelier
White metal with pewter wash and intricate detail.
Slip shades are white frosted. $999 - $1,150

1930s Five-Light Candle Chandelier
White metal with gold-tone wash. Intricate detail throughout. $599 - $725

1930s Six-Light Candle Chandelier
White metal with gold-tone finish. Five frosted panels at center surround center light. $499 - $575

1930s Ceiling Fixture
Chrome ceiling canopy and housing. Fixture
white milk glass with clear pressed glass bottom.
39" high, glass fixture 11" high x 9" diameter.
$535 - $610

1930s Ceiling Fixture
White milk glass with detail throughout each panel.
$445 - $495

1940s Ceiling Pendant Fixture
Milk glass with embossed floral design at base.
$365 - $395

1940s Three-Light Chandelier
White metal with bronze wash. Intricate detail
throughout. Shades are white milk glass. $499 - $585

Chapter 4
Light Up!

Smoking tobacco was very fashionable in the 1920s through the 1940s. Ashtrays and smoking stands were common in public buildings, including doctors' offices, office buildings and banks, and in private homes. A few lighted smoking stands and ashtray lamps were manufactured for fashion conscious smokers. These utilitarian objects could also serve as sources of light.

1930s Smoking Stand with Lighted Base
Alabaster base and accents. White metal with
chrome plate. Smoking stand contains two ashtrays, cigarette lighter, and cigarette container. 28"
high x 9" square base. $495 - $610

1930s Floor Ashtray with Lighted Base
White metal with bronze wash. Lighted base of
alabaster and brass. 33" high x 8" diameter base.
$495 - $610

1930s Figural Ashtray Lamp
White metal with chrome plate. 5" wide x 10"
high. $400 - $550

1930s Nuart Figural Ashtray Lamp
White metal with black wash and glass ashtray
insert. Multi-colored glass globe of the deco period.
5 1/4" wide x 13 3/4" high. $590 - $685

 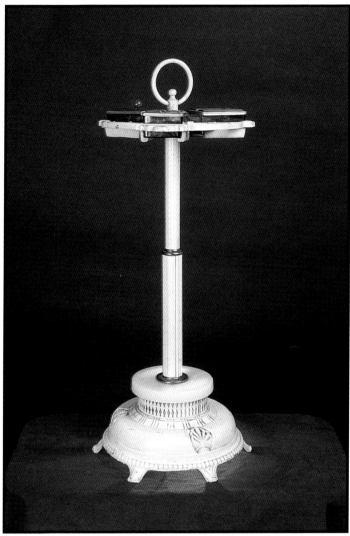

1940s Smoking Stand with Electric Lighter
Alabaster and chrome. Very unusual lighted base and top which display lighted stars
at top and bottom. Smoking stand contains an electric lighter, two ashtrays, and cigarette container. 29" high x 11 ½" diameter base. $510 - $625

1940s Smoking Stand with Lighted Base
White metal with cream wash. Lighted base is alabaster. Smoking stand contains two cobalt blue ashtrays with one cobalt blue glass cigarette box. All lids are chrome plated. - 29 ½" high x 8" diameter base. $465 - $535

CHAPTER 5
FLOOR LIGHTING

Many commercial venues found uses for floor lighting. Torchiere lamps were popular in funeral homes in the art deco era and remain so today. They were also found in sitting rooms of many homes and offices. Torchieres could light just one portion of a room or the entire room. Many were designed to accept a mogul base bulb, which is larger than the base of a standard electric light bulb. Mogul bulbs give from 100 to 350 watts of light. The lamps were usually manufactured with porcelain sockets which were designed to withstand the greater heat of the bulb with three-way switches.

Bridge lamps were designed to provide reading light next to a chair, sofa, or bed. Many were designed with architectural details, while others were simple in their designs.

1930s Floor Lamp
White metal with brass overlay
design. Shade and finial have been
replaced. 68" high x 9" diameter
base. $785 - $910

1930s Floor Lamp

White metal with cast iron base. Intricate design throughout. Floor lamp houses three candle-shaped bulbs. Unusual design with the upper portion of lamp separating from the base to be used as a walking torch. Lamp was formerly used in theaters by ushers to assist in seating. 60" high x 8 3/4" diameter base. $495 - $685

1930s European Bridge lamp
White metal with bronze wash and marble base. Bridge of lamp is sculptured as a griffin which holds a deco period glass shade. At center of lamp is a sculptured, two-sided women's face. Base of lamp has elaborate design and rests on marble base. 69" high x 9 3/4" diameter base. $1,135 - $1,250

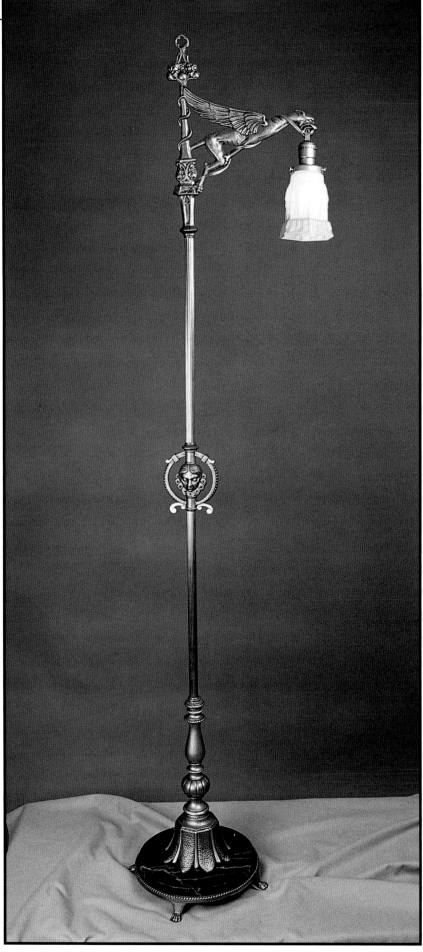

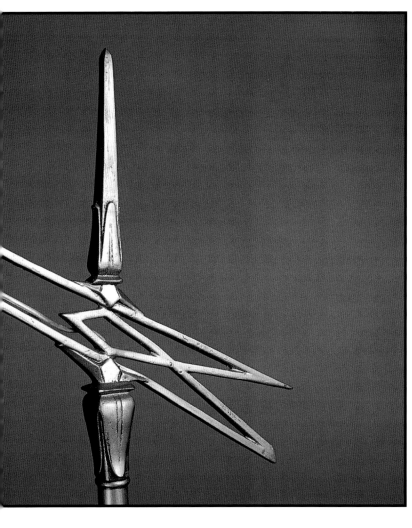

1930s Bridge Lamp
White metal. Architectural design at bridge and base. 62" high x 14" diameter base. New glass beaded shade. $865 - $999

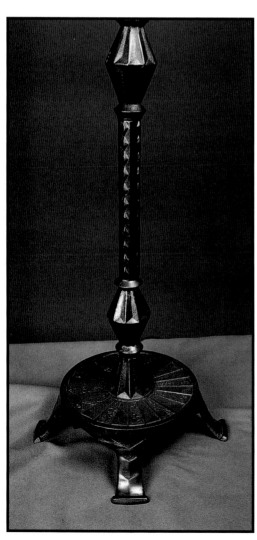

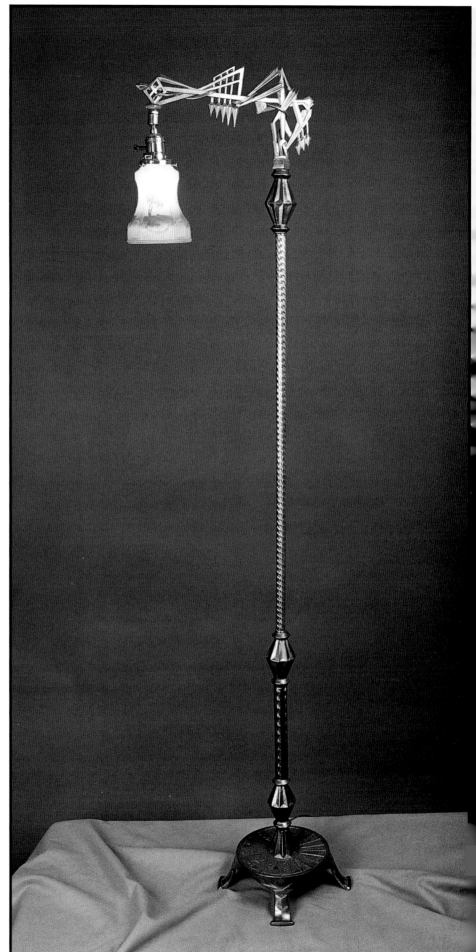

1930s Bridge Lamp
White metal with pewter wash. Architectural influence at
bridge. Deco period glass shade with palm trees. 62" high
x 8 1/2" diameter base. $565 - $650

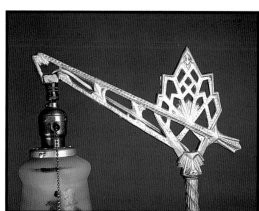

1930s Bridge Lamp
White metal with pewter finish. Multi-colored accents throughout column and base. Glass shade of the deco period. 57" high x 8 ¼" square base. $595 - $700

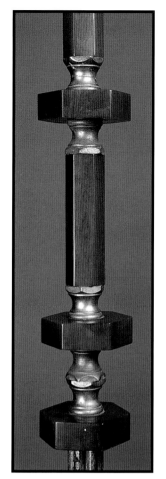

1930s Bridge Lamp
Bakelite on column of lamp. Base is marble on white metal. Shade is original paper. 58" high x 10" square base. $865 - $950

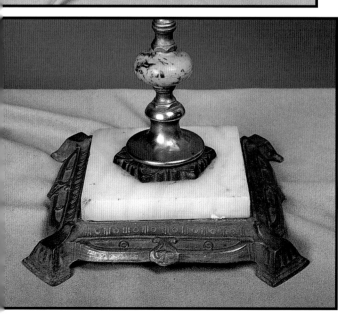

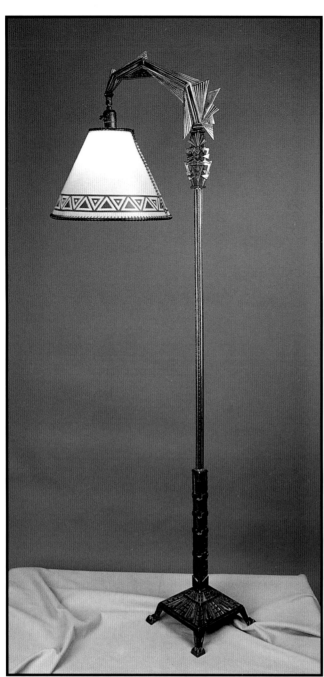

1930s Bridge Lamp
White metal with cast iron base with
architectural design. Paper shade of
the deco period. 66" high x 8 3/4"
square base. $1,165 - $1,450

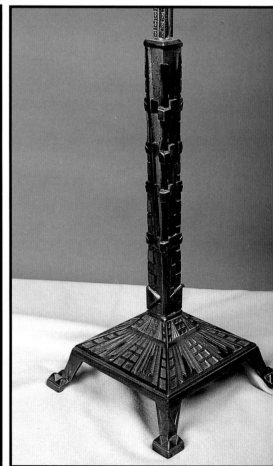

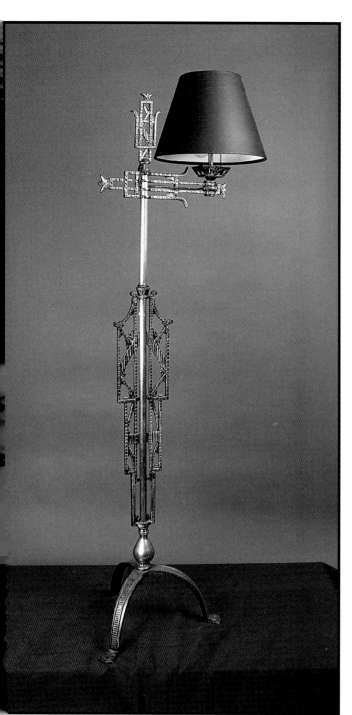

1930s Bridge Lamp
White metal with brass and pewter wash.
Shade has been replaced. 58" high x 14"
wide base. $545 - $650

1940s Bridge Lamp
White metal and chrome plate
with saturn base. Shade has been
replaced. 54" high x 7 1/2" diameter base. $465 - $525

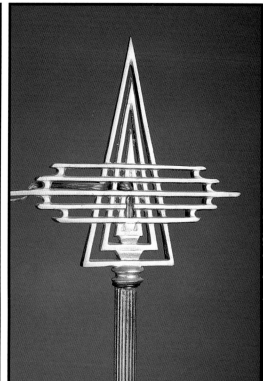

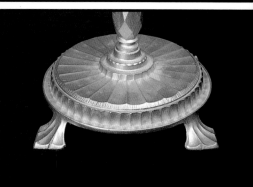

1940s Bridge Lamp
Brass and bronze wash. Glass shade of the deco period. 61 1/2" high x 12" diameter base. $485-$560

1920s Torchiere
Solid brass. Architectural influence in design. Original finish. Shades are original six-sided silk with original piping border. 65 1/2" high x 8 3/4" square base. $1,850 - $2,100 pair

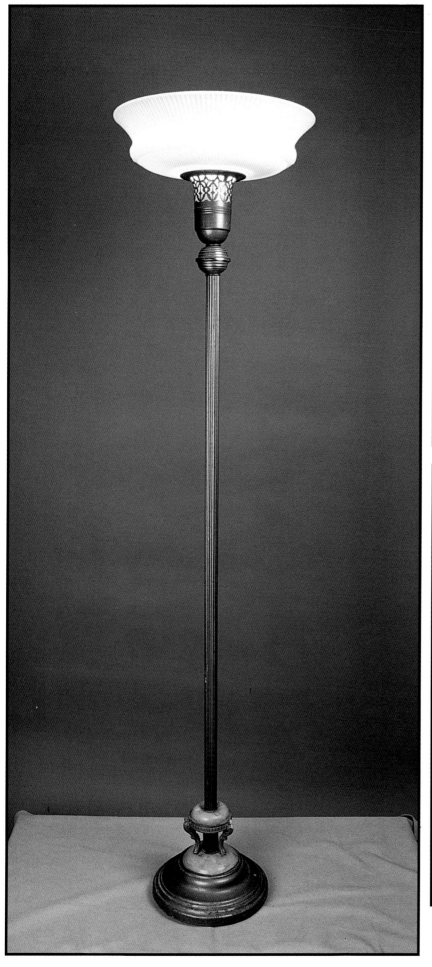

1930s Torchiere
White metal with bronze wash. Unusual
Bakelite lighted base with separate on/off
switch. Glass shade has been replaced. 65"
high x 10 3/4" diameter base. $685 - $750

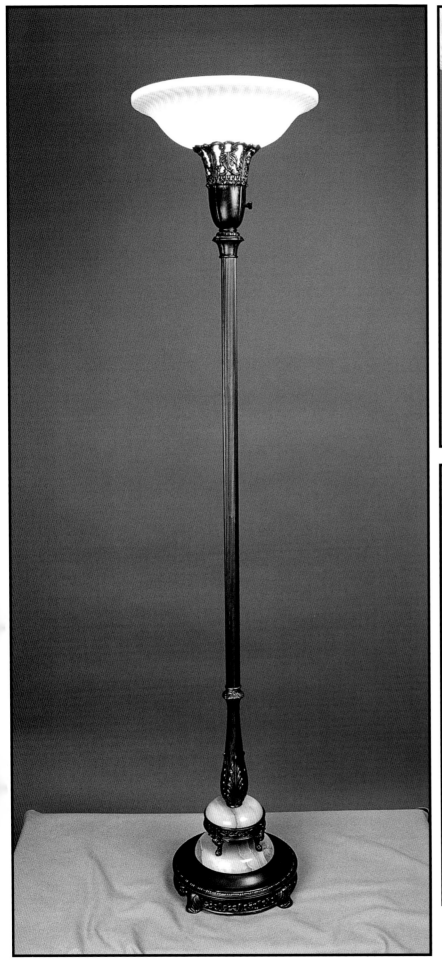

1930s Torchiere
White metal with bronze wash and two-tier
marble base. Glass shade has been replaced.
65" high x 9" diameter base. $710 - $795

1930s Torchiere
White metal with bronze wash. Lighted marble base with separate on/off switch. Glass shade has been replaced. 64" high x 9 1/4" diameter base. $685 - $740

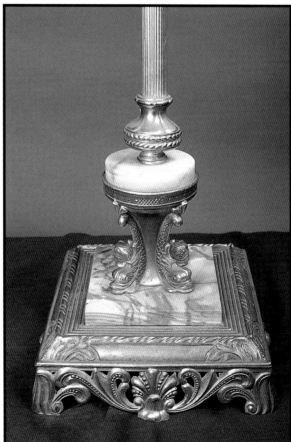

1930s   Torchiere
White metal with pewter wash. Base consists of both circular and square marble. Glass shade has been replaced. 69" high x 11" square base. $585 - $650

1930s Torchiere
White metal with bronze wash. Intricate deco design at fluted neck and base. White marble accent at base. 64" high x 8" diameter base. $585 - $650

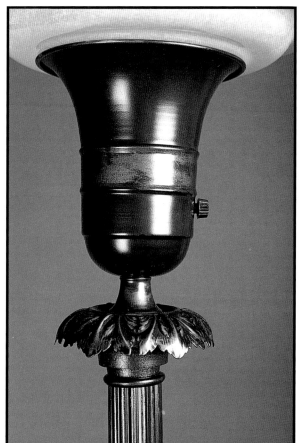

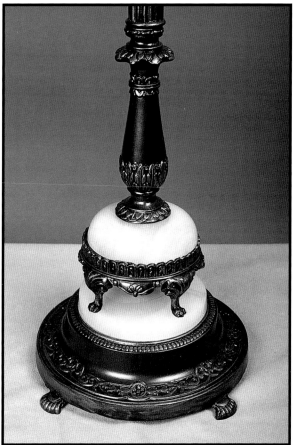

1930s Torchiere
White metal with bronze and copper wash. Two-tier white marble base. Glass shade has been replaced. 67" high x 8 3/4" diameter base. $685 - $775

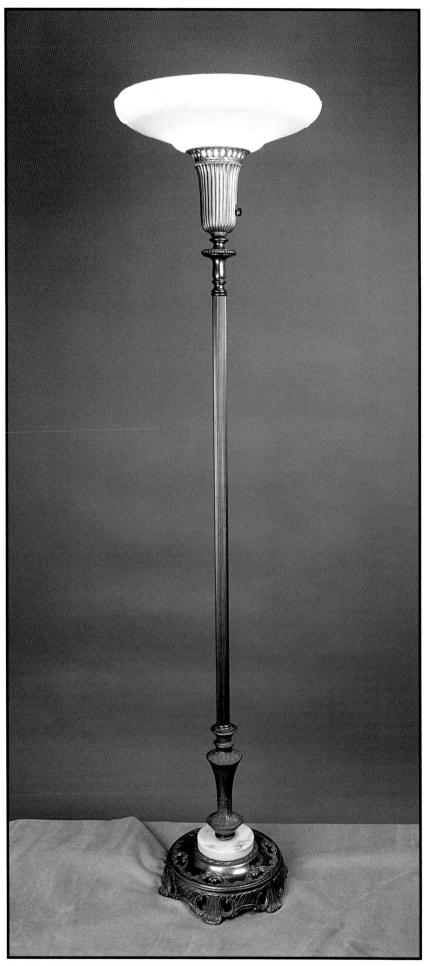

1930s Torchiere
White metal with bronze and brass wash.
Marble base. 64" high x 9 3/4" diameter
base. $495 - $565

Early 1940s Mini-Torchiere Lamps
Chrome plated with glass ball accent at base.
13" high x 4 3/4" diameter base. $315 - $450

1940s Torchiere
White metal with baked enamel bronze
finish and brass accents. Glass shade has
been replaced. 64 1/4" high x 11" diameter base. $465 - $525

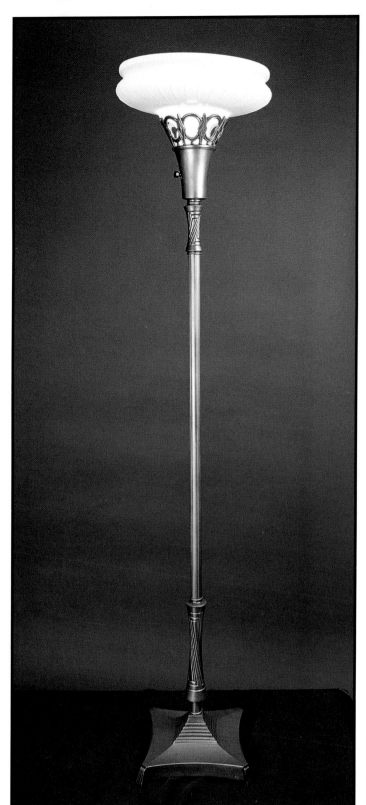

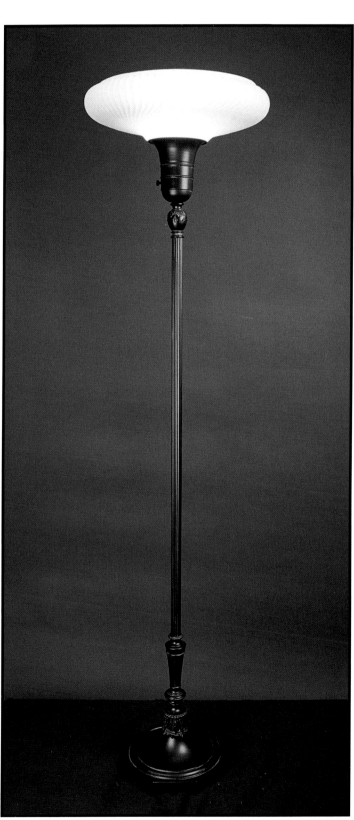

1940s Torchiere
White metal with brass finish. Glass shade has been replaced. 65" high x 8 3/4" square base. $465 - $525

1940s Torchiere
White metal with cast iron base and bronze wash. Glass shade has been replaced. 65" high x 8" diameter base. $495 - $550

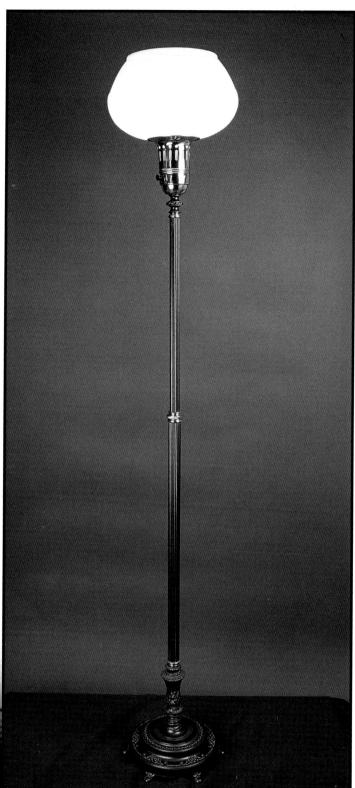

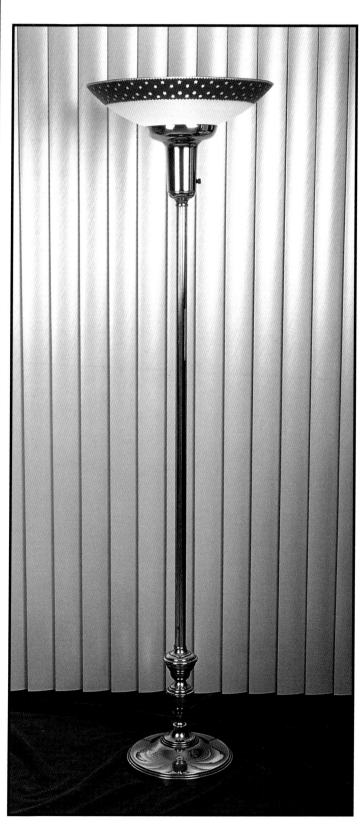

1940s Torchiere
White metal and cast iron base with bronze wash and brass accents. Unusual adjustments in height by turning center brass band. Glass shade has been replaced. 62" to 68" high. $525 - $610

1940s Torchiere
Chrome with glass shade of the deco period. White frosted glass with burgundy colored stars at upper border. $510 - $595

BIBLIOGRAPHY

Darton, Mike, *Art Deco - An Illustrated Guide to the Decorative Style 1920-1940*, North Deighton, Massachusetts: JG Press, 1996.

Duncan, Alastair, *Art Nouveau and Art Deco Lighting*, New York: Simon and Schuster, 1978.